To _____

FROM _____

DATE _____

WITH GOD ALL THINGS ARE POSSIBLE

WRITTEN & ILLUSTRATED BY
JOANNE FINK

HARVEST HOUSE PUBLISHERS
EUGENE, OREGON

WITH GOD ALL THINGS ARE POSSIBLE

This book was inspired by thoughts I wanted to share with my amazing children, Samantha & Jonathan Trattner, and is dedicated to them with love.

Text and art copyright © 2013 by Joanne Fink
Published by Harvest House Publishers
Eugene, Oregon 97402
www.harvesthousepublishers.com

ISBN 978-0-7369-4962-0

For more information on Joanne Fink, contact:
    Lakeside Design
    329 Nebraska Avenue
    Longwood, FL 32750
    Tel: 407.330.4465
    joanne@zenspirations.com
    www.zenspirations.com

Design and production by Lakeside Design, Longwood, Florida
Graphic design by Kimme Prindle, Lakeside Design
www.lakeside-design.com

Printed in China

13 14 15 16 17 18 19 20 21 / FC / 10 9 8 7 6 5 4 3 2 1

THE
TRUE COLORS
OF YOUR HEART
WILL
ILLUMINATE
THE
WORLD

NO MATTER
WHAT
NEVER,
NEVER
never
GIVE UP ON YOUR DREAMS

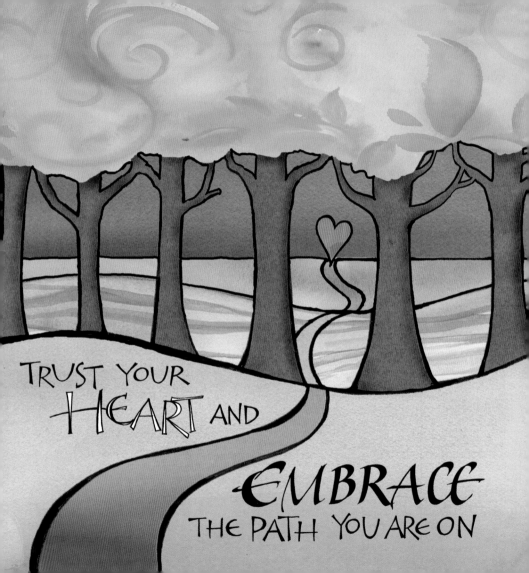

FOLLOW THE PATH YOUR HEART HAS EMBRACED AND YOU'LL ARRIVE AT THE PLACE YOUR SOUL CALLS HOME

Trust in the LORD

WITH ALL YOUR HEART AND LEAN NOT ON YOUR OWN UNDERSTANDING.

PROVERBS 3:5

YOU HAVE A
PURPOSE
FOR BEING
ON THIS EARTH
THAT IS FAR
MORE IMPORTANT
THAN ANYTHING
YOU HAVE EVER
DARED TO IMAGINE

A SINGLE LOVING ACT CAN TRANSFORM THE WORLD

LOVE CONNECTS

let it flow through you
inside you
and around you

LET
ALL YOU
DO COME
FROM A
PLACE OF
LOVE

DISCOVER
YOUR CONNECTION
TO THE DIVINE LIGHT
WHICH CONTINUALLY
BURNS IN YOUR SOUL

IT IS THE
LIGHT
OF PASSION

IT IS THE
LIGHT OF
Creativity

IT IS THE
LIGHT OF
LOVE

TRANQUILITY
GROWS
WITH THE
RECOGNITION
THAT YOUR
LIFE IS DIVINELY
PURPOSED

UNCAGE YOUR HEART SO YOUR SPIRIT CAN Soar

BE STILL
AND
KNOW
THAT
I AM
GOD.

PSALM 46:10

GREET EACH DAY WITH A HOPEFUL HEART

LOOK FOR
BEAUTY

LISTEN WITH
LOVE

LIVE WITH
INTENTION

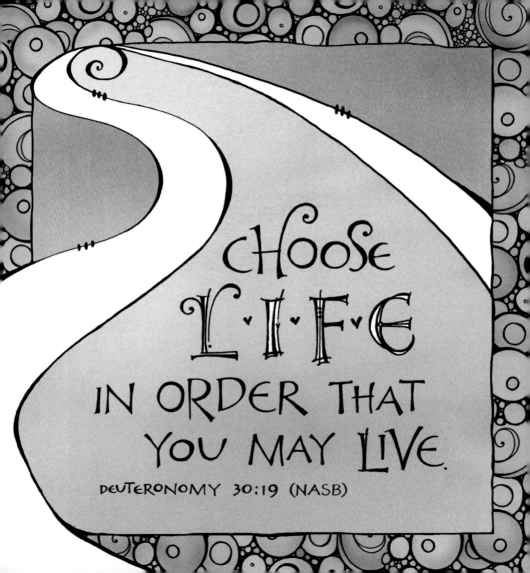

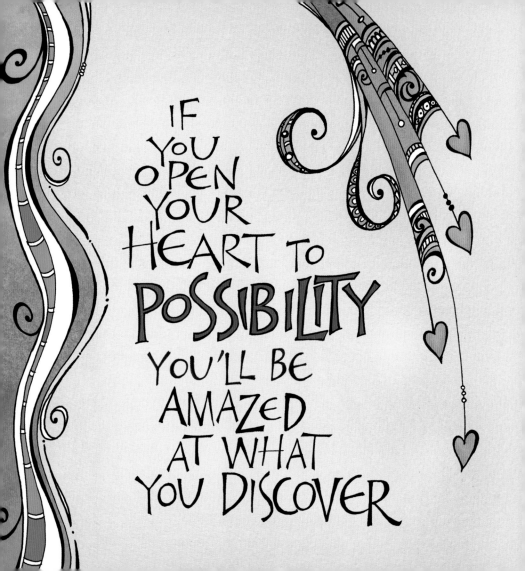

CELEBRATE
LIFE
GROWTH
&
POSSIBILITY

BLOOM

EACH
DAY IS AN
OPPORTUNITY
FOR A FRESH
START

focus ON THE POSITIVE

KEEP HOPING
KEEP SEARCHING
KEEP BELIEVING